THESE ARE OUR BODIES

FOR HIGH SCHOOL

Church Publishing
NEW YORK

PARTICIPANT BOOK

A catalog record of this book is available from the Library of Congress.

Church Publishing Incorporated
19 East 34th Street
New York, NY 10016

Cover design by: Jennifer Kopec, 2 Pug Design
Typeset by: Progressive Publishing Services

ISBN-13: 978-1-60674-333-1 (pbk.)
ISBN-13: 978-1-60674-334-8 (ebook)

Printed in the United States of America

CONTENTS

INTRODUCTION

Welcome to *These Are Our Bodies*!

We are so glad that you are in this program and that you have this *Participant Book*.

This book is your guide to use during each session of the program and for you to take home after the program is over. *These Are Our Bodies* is about connecting your faith life with your sexuality . . . this is very important and sometimes challenging. This book will help you during the program. It has prayers, Scripture, and reflection questions designed to help you see the connection between your sexuality and your spirituality.

By the end of our time together you will have the tools you need to be able to articulate your own Theology of Sexuality. As you take a critical look at the nature of God (theology) and relate it to your emotional, physical, and social well-being when it comes to matters of sex and sexuality, we hope you can better discern the ways in which God is calling you to be your full and authentic sexual, spiritual self.

A big goal of *These Are Our Bodies* is the formation of a group that provides a safe place for participants to honestly and openly engage the content of the program. In the church, when we do our most important work, we often form what are called *covenant groups*. Covenant groups form to help their members deal with difficult topics and grow together.[1] In Genesis, we learn that God formed a covenant with Noah and set the rainbow in the sky as a reminder of that covenant. We hear how God called Abraham to be the father of many nations and worked through Moses to deliver the People of Israel to the Promised Land. In the New Testament, Jesus gave us a new promise—that nothing can separate us from God.

> In the New Covenant, Jesus Christ reveals our sexuality as good, refocusing relationships to mutuality, respect, compassion, and hospitality. In the words of the Standing Commission on Liturgy and Music, "Baptism and Eucharist, as sacraments of God's covenant of creating, redeeming, and sustaining love, shapes our lives as Christians in relation to God and to God's creation; this calls us to live with love, compassion, justice, and peace toward all creatures, friend or foe, neighbor or stranger."[2]

As Episcopalians, our Baptismal Covenant[3] guides us in our beliefs as well as our behavior toward neighbor and self. In *These Are Our Bodies*, we see covenants as promises between leaders, parents, and participants as an important part of the program.

....

1   This theme of *covenant* not only informs our group ground rules for the program, it encompasses an overarching ethic of love, grace, and compassion at the foundation of the teaching and our lives as faithful people.

2   Leslie Choplin and Jenny Beaumont. *These Are Our Bodies: Talking Faith & Sexuality at Church & Home, Foundation Book* (New York: Church Publishing, 2016), 14.

3   Book of Common Prayer, 304–305.

In the context of *These Are Our Bodies*, the covenants are between the facilitators, participants, and their adults. We will go over each aspect of the RESPECT[4] covenant:

- R = take RESPONSIBILITY for what you say and feel without blaming others. We want to hear about your experiences and those of the other youth, and we ask that if you are telling about an experience that you leave the names out of the story, which will protect privacy. We also ask that you keep what the other participants say in this room. We do want you to share the good things you are learning, but leave names and other identifiers out of your stories.

- E = use EMPATHETIC listening. This way of listening involves seeking understanding and is built on respect. When we listen empathetically we pay attention to what others are saying, considering especially the emotions involved. We seek to respond in a compassionate way with feeling and insight into their perspective.

- S = be SENSITIVE to differences in communication styles. Each of us feels comfortable communicating in a different way. Some are more reflective and hesitant to disclose thoughts to the group. Some are external processors and like to speak what they are thinking as they think it. We seek to respect the differences in communication styles while encouraging all to participate fully in the way they feel most comfortable.

....

4 These "Respectful Communication Guidelines" were developed by Eric H. F. Law and the Kaleidoscope Institute. Versions of this in English, Spanish, French, Korean, and Chinese can be found on their website, along with a further explanation of them. http://www.kscopeinstitute.org/respectful-communication-guidelines/

- P = PONDER what you hear and feel before you speak. We want you to use good listening skills to hear and respond to one another, both lovingly and respectfully. In *These Are Our Bodies*, honesty is important. Everyone will have questions, and the facilitators promise to answer questions honestly. They will give you the information you need in a way that you can understand. In return, you promise to be honest about your questions and your feelings.

- E = EXAMINE your own assumptions and perceptions. In *These Are Our Bodies*, being open is imperative for us to learn and grow. We want all of you to be open to each other and your facilitators. And we want to be open to the work of the Holy Spirit in and among us.

- C = keep CONFIDENTIALITY. The facilitator promises not to tell your parents what individual participants say or do. We also ask that you keep what the other participants say in the room. You may tell your adults what the entire group did and the facilitators may summarize a discussion to share with the parents. But everyone will keep names and other identifiers private. The facilitators will not tell your adults the details of any one participant. One of the underlying commitments adult volunteers make is to the safety of the youth in our care. When working with youth, leaders might wonder when the promise of confidentiality or privacy should be broken. The safety of the youth or of other people trumps confidentiality. If an adult leader suspects that anyone has been harmed, will be abused, will hurt themselves, or may cause harm to others, the leader should act immediately. Leaders have an obligation to report any suspected abuse or any suspicion that a youth might hurt themselves or others. In the case of suspected abuse or potential harm to themselves or others, leaders will report their concerns to both the clergy at the church and Child Protective Services.[5]

- T = TRUST ambiguity because we are not here to debate who is right or wrong. Some of the topics we cover will be based on scientific fact. The "T" in respect refers to the conversations we will have about belief systems and about our theology of sexuality.

The book has nine chapters, one for each session. You will use your *Participant Book* during the sessions to reflect on and record what you are thinking, feeling, and learning. We provide lots of space for you to write and doodle.

You will also find Scripture passages to read and contemplate along with questions for you to think over on your own time.

At the end of the book (pp. 65–86) is a Glossary. It has words that we use in the sessions and many words that are just plain good to know. Take a look—it might surprise you! After the sessions are over, the *Participant Book* is yours to take home.

There is also a *Parent Book* for an adult in your home to use. You might want to get together and ask each other questions about what you are discovering.

Remember, this book is *yours*! Use it! Write in it. Keep it to recall the activities you did and the things you learned.

....

5 The phone numbers for Child Protective Services can be found at https://www.childwelfare.gov/. Mandatory Reporter Laws for your state can be found at https://www.childwelfare.gov/topics/systemwide/laws-policies/state.

OUR
INTRODUCTION

You did not choose me but I chose you. And
I appointed you to go and bear fruit, fruit
that will last, so that the Father will give
you whatever you ask him in my name.
I am giving you these commands so that
you may love one another.

—John 15:16–17

WORSHIP

Almighty God, the fountain of all wisdom: Enlighten by your Holy Spirit those who teach and those who learn, that, rejoicing in the knowledge of your truth, they may worship you and serve you from generation to generation; through Jesus Christ our Lord, who lives and reigns with you and the Holy Spirit, one God, forever and ever. *Amen.*[6]

WORK

In this session you and your parents, guardians, or caregivers will be introduced to *These Are Our Bodies.* You will get an overview of the program. Also, you will have the opportunity to ask questions about what will be covered in subsequent sessions. As part of this session you will learn the regular rhythm of future sessions so you know what to expect. During the first session you will begin to consider how sexuality and spirituality intersect.

WORD

Read Luke 19:45–48. (CEB)

How This Is Related to Sexuality

Everywhere you look you can find "the church" talking about sex. There are so many mixed messages, many of them filled with shame and negativity, that it seems odd we would talk about sexuality in church in a positive way. In this passage from Luke, Jesus was upset with the state of things. In a similar way, we

6 "Collect for Education," Book of Common Prayer, 261.

might be upset about the way we have heard sexuality talked about by the church, our schools, parents, peers, or the media. In this program we won't be yelling and flipping tables, but we can work to remove some of the more harmful narratives about sexuality. In doing so, we can bring our whole selves to God. We can only approach our sexuality in a prayerful way when we openly and honestly talk about sexuality in church.

Other Bible References

Here are some other pieces of Scripture that might help you think about the importance of the intersection of spirituality and sexuality in a new way:

- Luke 2:41–52—The Boy Jesus in the Temple (your parents discussed this Scripture during the session)
- 1 Timothy 4:11–16—A Good Minister of Jesus Christ
- Ephesians 4:1–16—Unity in the Body of Christ

WONDER

Note: These questions won't be discussed in the large group, rather these are for your own personal reflection at a later time. You can write in this book, use the questions as prompts for your own journaling, or discuss them with your family over dinner.

Before you came to this class what did you think about the relationship between sexuality and spirituality?

The opening activity was called "An Interactive Museum." As everyone added their thoughts and ideas to the pages on the wall, you were given a glimpse into their thoughts, hopes, beliefs, and biases. How did it help you see the variety and diversity of the people and ideas in the room?

Can you take that understanding of others' perspectives out into the world with you? How?

You had an opportunity to listen to other people tell you what they think God has to do with sexuality. Were there any opinions that reinforced your perspective? That made you change your mind or altered your view?

The Bible passage you read told about a time when Jesus overturned tables in the temple in order to make room for people who wanted to worship and pray. Is there something in your life you need Jesus's help throwing away in order for you to be closer to God? Maybe there's something you need Jesus to bring to you instead.

If you had to explain this whole lesson to someone in one sentence, what would it be?

Questions to Ask Yourself

These are questions you might want to ask yourself now or you might want to save for later. Either way, they will help you to deepen your understanding and commitments. They might also help you address real-life situations as they arise.

- Are these concepts things you feel comfortable talking to your parents about?

- How will you respond when your parents ask you about sexuality and spirituality?

WORSHIP

Leader: The Lord be with you.
Participants: And also with you.
Leader: Let us pray.

From Psalm 139
O Lord, you have searched me and known me.
You know when I sit down and when I rise up;
　you discern my thoughts from far away.
You search out my path and my lying down,
　and are acquainted with all my ways.
Even before a word is on my tongue,
　O Lord, you know it completely.
You hem me in, behind and before,
　and lay your hand upon me.
Such knowledge is too wonderful for me;
　it is so high that I cannot attain it.

A Reading from Romans 12:2
Do not be conformed to this world, but be transformed by the renewing of your minds, so that you may discern what is the will of God—what is good and acceptable and perfect.

A period of silence may follow.

Prayers may be offered for ourselves and others.

The Lord's Prayer

Our Father, who art in heaven,
    hallowed be thy Name,
    thy kingdom come,
    thy will be done,
        on earth as it is in heaven.
Give us this day our daily bread.
And forgive us our trespasses,
    as we forgive those
        who trespass against us.
And lead us not into temptation,
    but deliver us from evil.
For thine is the kingdom,
    and the power, and the glory,
    for ever and ever. Amen.

The Collect

O God, you made us in your own image and redeemed us through Jesus your Son: Look with compassion on the whole human family; take away the arrogance and hatred which infect our hearts; break down the walls that separate us; unite us in bonds of love; and work through our struggle and confusion to accomplish your purposes on earth; that, in your good time, all nations and races may serve you in harmony around your heavenly throne; through Jesus Christ our Lord. *Amen.*[7]

---

7 "Prayer for the Human Family," Book of Common Prayer, 815.

OUR
LANGUAGE

Desire without knowledge is not good,
and one who moves too hurriedly misses the way.
—Proverbs 19:2

WELCOME

Read the Collect for Education found on page 11 of this book.

WORK

In this second lesson, you will learn some vocabulary about sexuality. But first we want to know what kind of words you use or know already. We will work on building a common vocabulary so that we are all on the same page and can fully comprehend what each other is saying. We hope by naming some of these things, both the clinical terminology and the slang, we will ease some of your anxiety and relieve some of the stigma of talking openly about sexuality.

WORD

Read Ephesians 4:25–32. (NRSV)

How This Is Related to Sexuality

When we were younger we would say, "Sticks and stones may break my bones but words will never hurt me." How much do we wish that were still true today? Words said in anger or with malice can cause wounds much worse than a broken bone. In this reading, Paul isn't telling us we can never get angry, but he is reminding us that we can express all of our emotions in ways that build up instead of tear down.

In a similar way, vocabulary around sexuality can be shocking for some people, especially out of context. That's why words related to sex make such powerful insults. If we are to "be kind to one another," we can work to use words correctly and gently correct those around us to do the same. We are also able to know each other more fully when we are specific and particular in our language use.

Other Bible References

Here are some other pieces of Scripture that might help you think about the importance of the way we use language in a new way:

- Matthew 18:15–20—Reproving Another Who Sins
- John 1:1–5—The Word Became Flesh

WONDER

What words or phrases come to mind when you think about sexuality?

During the activity we brainstormed lots of words and phrases. Were there any that surprised you? Any that you hadn't heard before?

Are there any words or phrases we used that need more explanation? That you are still unclear about what they mean or refer to?

Language is a powerful thing. When choosing which words to use as a group, were there any big disagreements? Which words were the most contentious? How did you come to a consensus?

How can choosing your words carefully when talking about sexuality help bring spirituality into the conversation?

Questions to Ask Yourself

These are questions you might want to ask yourself now or you might want to save for later. Either way, they will help you to deepen your understanding and commitments. They might also help you address real-life situations as they arise.

- What words do I use to describe my own body? My sexuality?
- What words do I use to describe others' bodies? Others' sexuality?
- What words or phrases cause me discomfort? Why?
- What words or phrases regarding sexuality offend me?
- How will I tell someone that their language bothers me?
- How will I tell someone how I want to be spoken about?

WORSHIP

Refer to page 15 for concluding prayers with this Scripture reading:

A Reading from Proverbs 19:2

OUR VALUE SYSTEM

Finally, beloved, whatever is true,
whatever is honorable, whatever is just,
whatever is pure, whatever is pleasing,
whatever is commendable, if there is any
excellence and if there is anything worthy of
praise, think about these things.
—Philippians 4:8

WELCOME

Read the Collect for Education found on page 11.

WORK

In Session 3 you will talk about where your values come from and who or what teaches them to you. We receive messages about what is right and wrong or good and bad from many sources in our lives. In this session you will work to claim your own values by thinking critically about what you actually believe to be good or bad, right or wrong. When your values are well defined, it makes making decisions about your sexuality much clearer and easier.

WORD

Read Romans 7:14–25. (NRSV)

How This Is Related to Sexuality

Temptation is everywhere. David fell prey to it. Jesus wrestled with it. And here, Paul struggles with it. We are taught by our parents and youth ministers and teachers the choices God wants us to make. Society also tries to influence our decisions and values. How do we discern for ourselves what is right? How do you trust your gut? How do you know what God wants for you? Is it possible to live a holy life, in communion with God, and also be a sexual being? How can you use your sexuality, your whole self, in a way that glorifies who God made you to be?

Other Bible References

Here are some other pieces of Scripture that might help you think about personal and cultural values in a new way:

- 2 Samuel 11–12:15—David and Bathsheba and Nathan
- Matthew 4:1–11—Jesus in the Wilderness
- Colossians 3:1–17—The New Life of Christ

WONDER

During the first activity, as you thought about what the different influences in your life say about some of the issues surrounding sex and sexuality, were there any answers that surprised you? How did they surprise you? Were your surprises based on assumptions you had made or misinformation you had been given?

When I was a child, I spoke like a child, I thought like a child, I reasoned like a child; when I became an adult, I put an end to childish ways. (1 Corinthians 13:11)

In what ways do you feel yourself putting away childish ways? How has your reasoning changed in the last year or so?

Do you ever feel like adults don't treat you in age-appropriate ways? How can you show the adults in your life your mature decision-making skills?

When you know something is wrong and do it anyway, or you know something is right but fail to do it, how does it affect your self-esteem?

What are some of your personal values regarding sexuality? (Remember, they may change throughout your life.)

What would it take for you to do a better job of matching your actions to your values?

Do you think it's even possible for someone to make the right decision all of the time? Why?

Questions to Ask Yourself

These are questions you might want to ask yourself now or you might want to save for later. Either way, they will help you to deepen your understanding and commitments. They might also help you address real-life situations as they arise.

- How will I take what other people say and incorporate or discern how their messages hold up to my own value system?
- What will I do to make things right when I make a bad decision?
- How can I refrain from forcing my own value system onto other people?
- How can I be a good role model for others?

WORSHIP

Refer to page 15 for concluding prayers with this Scripture reading:

A Reading from Philippians 4:8

OUR IDENTITY

For it was you who formed my inward parts;
you knit me together in my mother's womb.
I praise you, for I am fearfully and wonderfully made.
Wonderful are your works;
that I know very well.
My frame was not hidden from you,
when I was being made in secret,
intricately woven in the depths of the earth.
Your eyes beheld my unformed substance.
In your book were written
all the days that were formed for me,
when none of them as yet existed.
—Psalm 139:13–16

WELCOME

Read the Collect for Education found on page 11.

WORK

In Session 4 we will explore the multiplicity and complexity of our identities as sexual beings. You will be asked to think about your own identity and orientation. This may be something you have thought about before or it may be new territory. We will take some time to talk about what we present on the outside compared to who we actually are on the inside and how we can align these realities. Remember, your identity might shift and change throughout your life and that is perfectly normal.

WORD

Read 1 Corinthians 12:12–27. (NRSV)

How This Is Related to Sexuality

There are at least two ways to hear this reading. One is to take the almost literal description of your own body. How do all the parts of you—physical, mental and spiritual—play a part in making up your whole self? Remembering that we are interconnected, as one part of you changes or grows, the other parts are affected. Each part is of equal import and created specially by God. Remember that God loves your whole self even when you don't.

A second way to look at this passage is as if the church is the body and we are all parts within it. We are all connected in the body of Christ. So, even though at times it may feel like that one annoying person you know *has* to be the appendix (utterly useless until it tries to kill you), they, too, are worthy of honor and dignity. God is honored when we lift up the lowly. When we allow everyone to claim the dignity that God has given them, they are better able to live into who God called them to be.

Other Bible References

Here are some other pieces of Scripture that might help you think about identity and orientation in a new way:
- Genesis 25:19—Jacob and Esau
- Genesis 37—Joseph's coat and his brothers' hate
- Matthew 17:1–13—The Transfiguration

WONDER

In the activity, we talked about lots of different spectrums: gender, gender expression, sex, sexual attraction, romantic attraction. Have you considered how all of these things relate to you before this session?

Were there any ways of describing sexuality that you had never heard of before?

How would you describe yourself in relation to each . . . ?
- Gender
- Gender expression
- Sex
- Sexual attraction
- Romantic attraction

How do you want to be known by others?

What does it feel like when someone assumes things about you from the outside?

What does it feel like when someone really knows you as your authentic self?

What do you do in your life to try to know others more fully?

Questions to Ask Yourself

These are questions you might want to ask yourself now or you might want to save for later. Either way, they will help you to deepen your understanding and commitments. They might also help you address real-life situations as they arise.

- If you need to "come out" about an aspect of your identity to your friends and family, how will you decide how and when to do so?
- Who in your support system loves you unconditionally? How can you nurture these relationships?
- What role models do you have who share your identity and orientation?
- What will you do if a friend "comes out" to you?
- How will you work toward living an authentic and integrated life?

WORSHIP

Refer to page 15 for concluding prayers with this Scripture reading:

A Reading from Psalm 139:13–16

SESSION 5

OUR
SELF-IMAGE

Then God said, "Let us make humankind
in our image, according to our likeness; and let
them have dominion over the fish of the sea, and
over the birds of the air, and over the cattle, and
over all the wild animals of the earth, and over
every creeping thing that creeps upon the earth."
—Genesis 1:26

WELCOME

Read the Collect for Education found on page 11.

WORK

In Session 5 we will cover body and self-image. As we grow up we learn things from the world about what bodies should be, look, or act like. The truth is that we are made in the image of God just as we are meant to be. There is no *should*. Your body is beautiful and unique. We must teach ourselves self-acceptance and self-love. This also includes accepting and loving others just as they are because they are also made in God's image.

WORD

Read Genesis 3:1–11. (NRSV)

How This Is Related to Sexuality

A lot of small children (2- or 3-year-olds) go through what some parents call a "naked phase," when they never want to wear clothes. Negotiations occur over certain times and places when nudity is allowed (almost certainly not when guests come for dinner). The phase is naturally outgrown in a few months, but sometimes it ends abruptly as the child is taught, often unintentionally by a well-meaning adult, that what they are doing is wrong. This is just one example of the many ways we learn what is good or bad, right or wrong, when it comes to our bodies and ourselves.

What does the voice in your head sound like? It may sound like the snake, tempting you into shame and fear, or a parent or adult criticizing something you've done, or a peer commenting on your physical appearance. God offers a gentle, loving voice asking us, "Who told you that?" God does not want us to hide ourselves. How can we unlearn the harmful self-image we have internalized?

Other Bible References

Here are some other pieces of Scripture that might help you think about body and self-image in a new way:

- Luke 17:11–19—Jesus Heals Ten Lepers
- Galatians 3:23–29—The Purpose of the Law
- Luke 19:1–10—Jesus and Zacchaeus

WONDER

What have you been taught about what a body should be, look, or act like?

What does your body do that makes you proud?

How do you see God's image reflected in your body?

How do you honor your body?

In what ways do you judge other people based on their bodies? How might you change this behavior?

Questions to Ask Yourself

These are questions you might want to ask yourself now or you might want to save for later. Either way, they will help you to deepen your understanding and commitments. They might also help you address real-life situations as they arise.

- How will you respond if someone body-shames you?

- How can you consume media in a more critical way so that you are aware of the underlying messages it sends about body and self-image?
- Do you know what the signs are of an eating disorder or body dysmorphia? Do you know how to ask for help?

WORSHIP

Refer to page 15 for concluding prayers with this Scripture reading:

A Reading from Genesis 1:26

SESSION 6

OUR
RELATIONSHIPS

So then, putting away falsehood, let all of us speak
the truth to our neighbors, for we are members
of one another.
—Ephesians 4:25

WELCOME

Read the Collect for Education found on page 11.

WORK

In Session 6, we will explore relationships. We will be discussing both the positive and negative dynamics that arise in relationships. We will talk about all types of relationships: friendships, families, and romantic situations. You will learn about healthy relationship dynamics. When we or those we are close to are in unhealthy relationships we may not be sure how to create change. When we can name the positive dynamics to look for we can begin to incorporate them into our own relationships. Relationships take work. Part of being in relationship is having healthy communication skills. This takes practice.

WORD

Read 1 Corinthians 13. (CEB)

How This Is Related to Sexuality

In this passage we hear many descriptions of love. If we believe that God is love and we believe that we are made in the image of God, then we are called to emulate this love. This reading is almost always read at weddings when two people are making their commitment to each other public and permanent. We do so as a reminder to strive to love each other as God loves us. This takes work. When we are in relationship with others we must communicate what we need and what we are capable of giving.

If faith, hope, and love are the three things that remain, how does this frame who you are as a sexual being? There is a mutuality of trust that two people enter into when in relationship. Using this passage as a guide, we can work to be giving and respectful in all of our relationships and are free to expect the same from others.

Alternative Reading of 1 Corinthians

- *I am* patient,
- *I am* kind,
- *I am not* jealous,
- *I don't* brag,
- *I am not* arrogant,
- *I am not* rude,
- *I do not* seek *my* own advantage,
- *I am not* irritable,
- *I don't* keep a record of complaints,
- *I am not* happy with injustice,
- but *I am* happy with the truth.
- *I* put up with all things,
- *I* trust in all things,
- *I* hope for all things,
- *I* endure all things.

Other Bible References

Here are some other pieces of Scripture that might help you think about relationships and communication in a new way:

- 1 John 4:7–21—God is Love
- John 15:12–17—Love one another
- Acts 2:1–13—The coming of the Holy Spirit
- Judges 16—Samson and Delilah

WONDER

What was the experience of role-playing like?

In what ways are you an unhealthy communicator?

In what ways are you a healthy communicator?

What are some communication skills you like to use?

How does the love you show in relationships reflect the love God has for you?

How is God calling you to be in relationship to others?

Questions to Ask Yourself

These are questions you might want to ask yourself now or you might want to save for later. Either way, they will help you to deepen your understanding and commitments. They might also help you address real-life situations as they arise.

- What do you want in a relationship?
- What do you need in a relationship?

- What would you do if you found yourself in an unhealthy relationship? Who would you turn to for help?
- What will you do if you think a friend is in an unhealthy relationship?
- How will you break up with someone if and when you need to?

WORSHIP

Refer to page 15 for concluding prayers with this Scripture reading:

A Reading from Ephesians 4:1–3

SESSION 7

OUR HEALTH

Knowledge is powerful and empowering.
For wisdom will come into your heart,
and knowledge will be pleasant to your soul;
prudence will watch over you;
and understanding will guard you.
—Proverbs 2:10–11

WELCOME

Read the Collect for Education found on page 11.

WORK

In Session 7, you will gain tools to be able to own and take charge of your sexual health. There is far too much information regarding sexual health to cover in one session. In this session, you will gain more awareness about sexual health. But we will not be able to teach you everything you need to know. You should seek out more information in a way that you see fit whether through school, parents, your doctor, or a trusted website.

WORD

Read Matthew 13:10–17. (NRSV)

How This Is Related to Sexuality

Jesus speaks to us in parables that are often confusing and have many layers of meaning. The disciples approach him, asking why he teaches in this way. His answer is so that they might understand deeply and fully. In this same way, talking about sexuality is nuanced and complex. But we have eyes to see and ears to listen and so we are tasked with being filled with knowledge. Talking about sex can be awkward and weird. Sometimes talking about sex makes us want to shut our eyes, put our fingers in our ears, and yell, "La-la-la-la I can't hear you." This is basically what Jesus says people do in the Scripture.

True, some things we will learn by experience. Like figuring out just how spicy is too spicy. But we can use lessons from others to better understand what spicy means before we take a giant bite of that pepper. The adults who care for us want us to stay safe and to make wise choices. Right now, who do you think would give you the best advice that could keep you safe, help you make good choices, and who you would really, truly listen to?

Other Bible References

Here are some other pieces of scripture that might help you think about sexual health in a new way:

- Acts 10:15—Pure and Impure
- Matthew 15:10–20—Things That Defile
- Proverbs 2:10–11—Wisdom Will Guard You

WONDER

What did you already know about sexual health? STIs? Contraception?

What was new information for you?

From whom and where did you learn about sexual health?

How will the choices you make affect your sexual health?

Whom do you trust to talk to about your sexual health?

What would it look like for you to align your knowledge of sex and sexual health with your spirituality?

Which of the four information sources discussed in this session (Friends, Caregivers, A Trusted Adult, the Internet) will you go to for help when . . .

- Your boyfriend/girlfriend is pressuring you into performing or receiving oral sex
- You find a lump on your breast or testicle
- One of your caregivers walks in on you masturbating
- You have severe pain in your pelvic area
- You're embarrassed by the way your genitals appear
- You think you (or your girlfriend) are pregnant
- You have an itchy rash near your penis/vagina
- You want to begin taking birth control pills
- Your friend is asking you to go with them to get an abortion
- You're thinking about having sex for the first time
- Other scenarios you may have discussed in class

Which friends do you trust the most with this? Which adults do you know who will help you? Which websites have the most accurate information on these subjects?

Questions to Ask Yourself

These are questions you might want to ask yourself now or you might want to save for later. Either way they will help you to deepen your understanding and commitments. They might also help you address real-life situations as they arise.

- What will you do to protect yourself from harm?
- What questions do you need to ask a doctor?
- How will you know when you need to acquire contraception and which method will you choose?
- How will you talk to your parents about your sexual health?
- How will you talk to a partner about sexual health?

WORSHIP

Refer to page 15 for concluding prayers with this Scripture reading:

A Reading from Proverbs 2:10–11

SESSION 8

OUR
DIGNITY

He said to him, "'You shall love the Lord your God
with all your heart, and with all your soul, and
with all your mind.' This is the greatest and first
commandment. And a second is like it:
'You shall love your neighbor as yourself.'"
—Matthew 22:37–39

WELCOME

Read the Collect for Education found on page 11.

WORK

In Session 8, we will consider how we make decisions that respect the dignity of every human being. Whether or not we choose to respect the dignity of ourselves and others applies to both everyday interactions and important, life-changing events. We don't have control over how others move through the world, but we can choose how we respond to them. That being said, none of us is perfect. We live in a society where respecting dignity is not an integral part of our culture. Often, we have internalized so much negativity that participating in it becomes habitual. But making a bad choice does not make us bad people. Respecting the dignity of every human being is a lifelong pursuit and we must persist in living into this call.

WORD

Read Luke 8:40–56. (NRSV)

Read The Baptismal Covenant, which can be found on pages 304–305 of the Book of Common Prayer.

How This Is Related to Sexuality

It must have been difficult to come to Jesus for help. The man, Jairus, literally got on his knees to beg for help. The woman was so ashamed of her condition (in addition to that the fact that, as a woman, she wouldn't really be allowed to address a man so boldly) she felt the need to sneak her way to healing. Both of these people got what they came for, even though society dictated that they should be treated differently. Is there a chance that Jesus could have stopped his power from healing the woman who touched him in the crowd? Could he have kept walking, carrying her secret as his? Instead, he dignifies her need by praising her bravery and pointing to faith as the cause of her healing.

Jairus's daughter dies before Jesus can get to her. The crowd is told not to trouble Jesus any longer. As if the life of a young girl is too much trouble and not worth the bother. Once again, Jesus commands the narrative by imploring the crowd to simply believe. They had just seen a woman healed simply through the power of touch, why wouldn't his presence be capable of so much more?

In our Baptismal Covenant we are asked, "Will you . . . respect the dignity of every human being?" Our answer is "I will, with God's help." What kind of help do you need from God to be able to stand up for those around you who need defending? We can use kind words, communicate our needs clearly, and hold tight to our values while respecting the dignity of every human being.

Other Bible References

Here are some other pieces of Scripture that might help you think about respecting the dignity of every human being in a new way:
- Luke 7:36–50—A Woman Washes Jesus's Feet
- John 8:1–11—Jesus and the Woman Caught in Adultery
- Matthew 22:37–39—The Greatest Commandment

WONDER

How do you respect the dignity of others?

How do you respect your own dignity?

How do you respond when someone does not respect your dignity?

How do you respond when someone does not respect the dignity of someone else?

What can we see in Jesus's example of how to respect the dignity of all?

How will you account for your dignity when making choices about your sexuality?

Questions to Ask Yourself

These are questions you might want to ask yourself now or you might want to save for later. Either way, they will help you to deepen your understanding and commitments. They might also help you address real-life situations as they arise.

- What will you do when you realize you have made a choice that does not respect the dignity of yourself or others?
- How will you ask for and provide consent?

WORSHIP

Refer to page 15 for concluding prayers with this Scripture reading:

A Reading from Matthew 22:37–39

OUR
THEOLOGY

And when you turn to the right or when you turn to
the left, your ears shall hear a word behind you,
saying, "This is the way; walk in it."
—Isaiah 30:21

WELCOME

Read the Collect for Education found on page 11.

WORK

In Session 9, you will have the chance to look back on what you have learned throughout the different sessions. We will have some time individually to reflect on many aspects of ourselves as spiritual, sexual beings. You will reflect on what your guiding principles are, who or what resources you have to rely on, how you will make decisions, and more. At the end of this session you will be equipped to bring what you have learned into your daily life.

Your Temple

Foundation: What are your basic beliefs, driving statements about your theology of sexuality? (For example: "My body is a temple." "Respect the dignity of every human being." "Love God, Love Your Neighbor.")

Walls: Who are the people and what are the places you will turn to as resources or in times of need? (For example: doctor, caregiver, teacher, youth minister, priest, family member, friends, internet, or what I see on TV.)

Roof: How will you make decisions about your sexuality? (For example: I will ask for guidance, I will reflect on the theology of sexuality, I will take my time and think it out.)

Interior: What kind of godly sexual human will you be? (For example: kind, compassionate, respectful, independent, wise, I would like to be in charge of my own body.)

Exterior: What do I still need to figure out? (For example: What questions do you still have? What do you need to learn about yourself?)

WORD

Read John 14:1–14. (CEB)

How This Is Related to Sexuality

This is the last class of *These Are Our Bodies*. You may feel a little bit like Thomas, wondering how you can figure out the way forward after all of this. You may feel a little like Philip, needing just that one last (impossible) bit of knowledge before you go. There is only so much that we have been able to cover in our time together. The rest you must figure out with the tools you've acquired. The adults who have spent this time with you, other adults you trust, the friends you've made in these classes, your peers, the internet—all can help with continued learning.

You are not alone in your worries. You are not the first person to face these challenges. Help is all around you if you know who to ask and where to look. God has given you a great crowd of help ready to lift you up and show you the way. God is always with you.

Other Bible References

Here are some other pieces of Scripture that might help you think about when you are ready or your theology of sexuality in a new way:

- Hebrews 12:1—A great cloud of witnesses
- 1 Kings 3:5–14—Solomon asks for wisdom
- Song of Solomon 2:7—Do not awaken love until it is ready
- Isaiah 30:21 – God will show you the way

WONDER

Which parts of your temple feel more aspirational than real to you right now?

What is the greatest takeaway you have from this program?

How is your sexuality like a temple?

How is God present with you in your sexuality?

What is your theology of sexuality?

How will you claim your rightful place as a sexual, spiritual being?

After this program is over, how will you seek answers to your questions?

Questions to Ask Yourself

These are questions you might want to ask yourself now or you might want to save for later. Either way, they will help you to deepen your understanding and commitments. They might also help you address real-life situations as they arise.

- How will you remember and practice what you learned here?
- How will you take what you learned to help others?
- How will you know when you are ready to have sex, be in a relationship, etc.?

WORSHIP

Refer to page 15 for concluding prayers with this Scripture reading:

A Reading from Isaiah 30:21

And when you turn to the right or when you turn to the left, your ears shall hear a word behind you, saying, "This is the way; walk in it."

A period of silence may follow.

Prayers may be offered for ourselves and others.

Leader: As this is our last session together, I invite you to offer something that your learned by participating in *These Are Our Bodies* that you are grateful for.

The Lord's Prayer
Our Father, who art in heaven,
    hallowed be thy Name,
    thy kingdom come,
    thy will be done,
        on earth as it is in heaven.
Give us this day our daily bread.
And forgive us our trespasses,
    as we forgive those
        who trespass against us.
And lead us not into temptation,
    but deliver us from evil.
For thine is the kingdom,
    and the power, and the glory,
    for ever and ever. Amen.

The Collect
O God, you made us in your own image and redeemed us through Jesus your Son: Look with compassion on

the whole human family; take away the arrogance and hatred which infect our hearts; break down the walls that separate us; unite us in bonds of love; and work through our struggle and confusion to accomplish your purposes on earth; that, in your good time, all nations and races may serve you in harmony around your heavenly throne; through Jesus Christ our Lord.[8] *Amen.*

---

8 A prayer "For the Human Family," Book of Common Prayer, 815.

GLOSSARY

Authors' note: Many of these definitions were adapted from The Trevor Project, Planned Parenthood, Just Communities, LGBT Center UNC Chapel Hill,[9] Trans Student Educational Resources, and Merriam-Webster.

abortion. The termination and expulsion of a pregnancy before birth.

abortion pill. Popular term for mifepristone, a medication used to terminate pregnancy. (Mifeprex is the brand name.)

abstinence. The self-imposed practice of not doing something that a person wants to do. Sexual abstinence is the choice not to participate in some (or all) sexual activities.

affirmed female. Someone who identifies as female but was labeled male at birth.

affirmed male. Someone who identifies as male but was labeled female at birth.

agender: (1) An adjective describing a person who is internally ungendered or does not feel a sense of gender identity. (2) A person who is internally ungendered or does not have a felt sense of gender identity.

AIDS. Abbreviation for acquired immune deficiency syndrome, a disease caused by a virus that can be transmitted from an infected person to an uninfected person only by an exchange of blood, semen, vaginal mucus, urine, or feces; type of sexually transmitted infection.

ally. Someone who supports and stands up for the rights and dignity of individuals and identity groups other than their own. Someone who rejects the dominant ideology and takes action against oppression out of the belief that eliminating oppression will benefit all people in both privileged and target groups.

anal sex. Sex in which the penis enters the anus.

androgens. Certain hormones that stimulate male sexual development and secondary male sex characteristics. Large amounts are produced in men's testicles and small amounts are produced in women's ovaries. The most common androgen is testosterone.

androgyny. A gender identity that allows the expression of both gender roles.

anorexia. A person with anorexia nervosa may have an intense fear of gaining weight or getting fat. It is one of a number of eating disorders, including bulimia nervosa.

anus. The opening from the rectum from which solid waste (feces) leaves the body.

aromantic. Individuals who do not experience romantic attraction toward individuals of any gender(s).

asexuality. Having little to no interest in having sex, even though the person may desire emotionally intimate relationships. Asexual people are also known as "Ace" or "Aces."

assigned sex. Gender assigned at birth.

bigendered. Expressing femininity and masculinity at different times.

binary. Used as an adjective to describe the genders female/male or woman/man.

biological sex. How we are defined as female, male, or intersex. It describes our internal and external bodies, including our sexual and reproductive anatomy, our genetic makeup, and our hormones.

biromantic. Romantic attraction toward males and females.

birth control. Behaviors, devices, or medications used to avoid unintended pregnancy.

birth control implant. A tube that is placed under the skin of the upper, inner arm that prevents pregnancy for up to 3 years by releasing a hormone that prevents the ovaries from releasing eggs.

birth control patch. The birth control patch is a thin, beige, plastic patch prescribed by a doctor that sticks to the skin and is used to prevent pregnancy.

birth control pill. An oral contraceptive, often called "the pill." Hormones (like the ones already in a woman's body) that keep the ovaries from releasing eggs as long as she keeps taking them.

birth control ring. A ring that contains hormones and is inserted in the vagina to prevent pregnancy. The ring is a reversible hormonal method of birth control available only by prescription. Also called "NuvaRing."

birth control shot. The birth control shot is an injection of a hormone that prevents pregnancy. Each shot prevents pregnancy for 3 months and must be prescribed by a doctor.

bisexual. A person who has sexual desire for males and females.

body dysmorphia. Also known as Body Dysmporphic Disorder, or BDD, this is a body-image disorder characterized by persistent and intrusive preoccupations with an imagined or slight defect in one's appearance.

body image. The way you see yourself, imagine how you look, and feel about your body.

breast. Two glands on the chest of a woman. Like mammary glands in other mammals, they produce milk during and after pregnancy. Breasts are secondary sex characteristics in women as they are often sexually sensitive and may inspire sexual desire. Men also have breast tissue.

breast cancer. A type of cancer that develops in breast tissue. Signs of breast cancer may include a lump in the breast, a change in breast shape, dimpling of the skin, fluid coming from the nipple, or a red scaly patch of skin.

bulimia. An eating disorder characterized by binge eating followed by purging. Binge eating refers to eating a large amount of food in a short amount of time. Purging refers to the attempts to get rid of the food consumed. This may be done by vomiting or taking laxatives. Other efforts to lose weight may include the use of diuretics, stimulants, water fasting, or excessive exercise.

celibacy. Not having sex.

cervical cap. A firm, thimble-like, rubber or silicone cup that is intended to fit securely on the cervix. Used with contraceptive jelly, the cervical cap is a barrier method of birth control that is reversible and available only by prescription.

cervix. The narrow, lower part—neck—of the uterus, with a narrow opening connecting the uterus to the vagina.

chancroid. A once very common sexually transmitted bacterium that causes open genital sores, called buboes.

chlamydia. A common, sexually transmitted bacterium that can cause sterility and arthritis in women and men.

circumcision. An operation to remove the foreskin of the penis or the clitoral hood.

cis (gender). Someone who identifies with the gender they were given at birth. Most people who have female bodies feel like girls or women, and most people who have male bodies feel like boys or men. A cisgender/cis person is not transgender. "Cisgender" does not indicate biology, gender expression, or sexuality/sexual orientation. Cis is not a "fake" word and is not a slur.

clitoris. Small, cylinder-shaped organ located just above the urethra made of very sensitive tissue.

closeted/in the closet. Concealing one's true identity (especially bisexual, lesbian, gay, or transgender) from oneself and/or others.

come out. The process of accepting and being open about one's previously concealed identity, such as being bisexual, lesbian, gay, or transgender.

conception. The moment when the pre-embryo attaches to the lining of the uterus and pregnancy begins. Also used to describe the fertilization of the egg.

condom. A sheath worn over the penis to catch the semen during ejaculation; a form of birth control; can reduce the risk of contracting most sexually transmitted infections.

consent. An agreement between participants to engage in sexual activity.

contraception. Any behavior, device, medication, or procedure used to prevent pregnancy.

covenant. A contract or agreement, such as between God and God's people, or between individuals.

cyber bullying. Bullying that takes place using electronic technology, including devices and equipment such as cell phones, computers, and tablets, as well as communication tools, including social media sites, text messages, chat, and websites.

cybersex. Receiving sexual stimulation using online media, the internet, video cams, e-mail, or instant messaging.

cyberstalking. To track and follow someone's online presence and communications in a threatening way.

date rape. Sexual contact that is forced during a dating relationship.

demiromantic. An individual who does not experience romantic attraction until after a close emotional bond has been formed. People who refer to themselves as demi-romantic may choose to further specify the gender(s) of those they are attracted to (e.g., demi-homoromantic).

demisexual. Individuals who do not experience primary sexual attraction but may experience secondary sexual attraction after a close emotional connection has already formed.

diaphragm. A soft rubber dome intended to fit securely over the cervix and used with contraceptive cream or jelly, it is a reversible barrier method of birth control available only by prescription.

douche. A spray of water or solution of medication into the vagina.

egg. The reproductive cell in women; the largest cell in the human body.

ejaculation. Sudden pushing and squeezing action that forces semen from the penis during male orgasm.

embryo. The organism that develops from the pre-embryo and begins to share the woman's blood supply about 16–18 days after fertilization (7 to 8 days after implantation).

endometriosis. The growth of endometrial tissue outside of the uterus, causing pain especially before and during menstruation.

erection. Process by which the blood rushes into the penis causing it to enlarge and stiffen.

erotica. Sexually arousing imagery that is not considered pornographic, obscene, or offensive to the average person.

estrogen. A hormone commonly made in a woman's ovaries. Estrogen's major feminizing effects are seen during puberty, menstruation, and pregnancy.

fallopian tube. One of two narrow tubes that carry the egg from the ovary to the uterus.

female condom. A polyurethane pouch with flexible rings at each end that is inserted deep into the vagina like a diaphragm. It is an over-the-counter, reversible barrier method of birth control that provides protection against many sexually transmitted infections. May also be used for anal intercourse.

feminine. Characteristics and ways of appearing and behaving that a culture associates with being a girl or a woman.

fertility awareness based method. Ways to prevent or plan pregnancy by predicting ovulation based on understanding a woman's fertility cycle. These are reversible behavioral methods of birth control that include the calendar method, the cervical mucus method, the Standard Days method, the Two-Days method, and the temperature method. All but the Standard Days method require careful, professional instruction.

fertilization. The joining of an egg and sperm that forms the zygote.

fetus. The organism that develops from the embryo at the end of about 8 weeks of pregnancy (10 weeks since a woman's last menstrual period) and receives nourishment through the placenta.

flirting. A playful behavior intended to arouse sexual interest or to make playfully romantic or sexual overtures.

fondling. Touching a partner to give sexual pleasure.

foreplay. Physical and sexual stimulation—kissing, rubbing, stroking, and touching—that often happens in the excitement stage of sexual response. Foreplay often occurs before intercourse but can lead to orgasm without intercourse, in which case it is called outercourse.

foreskin. A retractable tube of skin that covers and protects the glans (head) of the penis.

gay. Homosexual, especially in regard to men.

gender. A socially determined way of describing human beings based on characteristics like appearance, dress, reproductive organs, and behavior, now thought of as a continuum or spectrum.

gender-affirming surgery. Surgery does not change one's sex or gender, only one's genitalia. Also known today as genital reconstruction surgery and genital reassignment surgery. The terms "sex change," "sex reassignment surgery," and "gender reassignment surgery" are considered inaccurate and offensive.

gender binary. A traditional understanding that one is either male or female based on one's chromosomal sex (XX—female/XY—male). This system is oppressive to anyone who defies their sex assigned at birth but particularly to those who are gender-variant or do not fit neatly into one of the two standard categories.

gender expression. How one conveys their gender and gender roles through clothing, behavior, and personal appearance.

gender fluid. An internal sense that someone does not feel like they fit into a specific category for gender. Describes someone who moves in and out of different ways of expressing and identifying themselves.

gender identity. One's perception of the social category to which they belong—being male, female, neither, or both. For example, a person can have a penis and testicles but not the internal sense that they are a man. That individual's gender identity might be described as female.

gender queer. An adjective used to describe a person who is part of a group of people who do not feel that they fit into the traditional two genders of a gender-binary system. As with any other group that aligns with transgender identities, the reasons for identifying as gender queer vary.

gender roles. Society's set of roles, values, and expectations for what it means to be a girl/woman or a boy/man in a particular culture. The U.S. culture recognizes two distinct gender roles: "masculine" (having the qualities or characteristics attributed to males) and "feminine" (having the qualities or characteristics attributed to females). In other words, what we learn from our culture about what a "real man" or a "real woman" is supposed to be/do. A third gender role, rarely condoned in our society, is androgyny, combining assumed male (*andro*) and female (*gyne*) qualities.

genetic makeup. Refers to whether scientific tests determine a person has XX, XY, or another makeup of chromosomes.

genitals. External sex and reproductive organs: the vulva in women, the penis and scrotum in men. Sometimes, the internal reproductive organs are also called genitals.

genital herpes. An infection of herpes simplex virus types 1 or 2 in the area of the anus, buttocks, cervix, penis, vagina, or vulva. Very often there are no symptoms, while the most common symptom is a cluster of blistery sores.

genital warts. Soft, flesh-colored growths caused by several types of the human papilloma virus. They may look like miniature cauliflower florets and are usually painless, but may itch.

gonorrhea. A sexually transmitted bacterium that can cause sterility, arthritis, and heart problems.

gynecology. Sexual and reproductive health care for women.

hepatitis B. An infection that can be sexually transmitted and may cause severe liver disease and death.

herpes. An infection of herpes simplex virus types 1 or 2 in the area of the anus, buttocks, cervix, mouth, penis, vagina, or vulva. Very often there are no symptoms, while the most common symptom is a cluster of blistery sores.

heteronormative. Denoting or relating to a world view that promotes heterosexuality as the normal or preferred sexual orientation.

heteroromantic. Romantic attraction toward person(s) of a different gender.

heterosexism. The belief that everyone is or should be heterosexual.

heterosexuality. Someone who has sexual desire for people of the other gender.

homoromantic. Romantic attraction towards person(s) of the same gender.

homosexuality. Romantic attraction, sexual attraction, or sexual behavior between members of the same sex or gender. A woman who is attracted to other women often calls herself *gay*, *lesbian*, or *homosexual*. A man who is attracted to other men often calls himself *gay* or *homosexual*.

hormones. Testosterone, progesterone, and estrogen are hormones connected to human sexuality.

human immunodeficiency virus (HIV). An infection that weakens the body's ability to fight disease and can cause AIDS.

human papillomavirus. Any of more than 100 different types of infection, some of which may cause genital warts. Others may cause cancer of the anus, cervix, penis, throat, or vulva.

hymen. A thin fleshy tissue that stretches across part of the opening to the vagina.

infatuation. Impulsive, usually short-lived, emotional, and erotic attachment to another person.

infertility. The inability to become pregnant or to cause a pregnancy.

infidelity. Failing to keep a promise to be monogamous.

intersex. An adjective describing a person with a less common combination of hormones, chromosomes, and anatomy that are used to assign sex at birth. It is a group of conditions in which there is discrepancy between the external genitals and the internal genitals (the testes and ovaries). About 4 percent of the population can be defined as "intersex." For example, a person might be born appearing to be female on the outside, but have mostly male anatomy on the inside. Or a person may be born with genitals that seem to be in between the usual male and female types. (*Note:* The word *hermaphrodite* is an archaic term from Greek mythology. It is offensive to intersex people.)

intimacy. The closeness and familiarity we feel as we share our private and personal selves with someone else.

IUD. Abbreviation for intrauterine device; a reversible type of birth control. A device that is implanted into the uterus in the doctor's office.

labia. Labia majora are the outer lips of the vulva and labia minora are the inner lips of the vulva.

lesbian. A woman who is attracted to other women often calls herself *gay*, a *lesbian*, or *homosexual*.

LGBTQ+. Indicates a collection of identities; an abbreviation standing for lesbian, gay, bisexual, transgender, queer, questioning, intersex, asexual, aromantic, pansexual. An inclusive term that seeks to capture all sexual and gender identities other than heterosexual. Sometimes this acronym is replaced with "queer." (*Note:* "Ally" is not included in the acronym by most.)

lust. Feeling of intense desire and attraction toward a person; the emotion of sex and sexual desire.

manual sex. Sex involving the hands, including handjobs and fingering.

masculine. Characteristics and ways of appearing and behaving that a culture associates with being a boy or a man.

masturbation. Touching, rubbing, or stimulating one's own sex organs, producing a pleasurable feeling and sexual excitement.

menopause. The time at "midlife" when menstruation stops; a woman's last period; usually occurs between the ages of 45 and 55. "Surgical" menopause, however, results from removal of the ovaries and may occur earlier.

menstrual cycle. The time from the first day of one period to the first day of the next period. In women of reproductive age, about 15–44, it is the period in which the lining of the uterus is shed whenever implantation does not happen, followed by the regrowth of the lining of the uterus in preparation for implantation. The discharge is called **menses**. The stage when this inner lining is shed is call **menstruation**.

miscarriage. The loss of a pregnancy before 20 weeks gestation—before the embryo or fetus can live outside the uterus.

molluscum congagiosum. A virus that can be sexually transmitted, causing small, pinkish-white, waxy, round, polyp-like growths in the genital area or on the thighs.

monogamy. A relationship in which both people date or have sex only with one another and no one else.

morning-after pill. Emergency hormonal contraception that is started within 120 hours (5 days) of unprotected vaginal intercourse to decrease the risk of unintended pregnancy.

nocturnal emission. Ejaculation of semen from the penis while a male is sleeping. Another name for this is *wet dream*. Only about a teaspoon of semen is released from the penis during ejaculation.

nonbinary sexual orientation. A way to describe attractions to people who do not identify as just male/man or female/woman. Examples of nonbinary sexual orientations include, but are not limited to, pansexual, bisexual, queer.

oral sex. Sex involving the mouth and genitals, including: cunnilingus, felattio, anilingus.

orgasm. The peak of sexual arousal when all the muscles that were tightened during sexual arousal relax, causing a very pleasurable feeling that may involve the whole body. The fourth stage of the sexual response cycle.

orientation. The determination of the relative position of something or someone (especially oneself).

out. Being open about one's own sexual orientation, intersex, or transgender status.

ovarian cancer. Ovarian cancer happens if abnormal cells in one or both of the ovaries grow uncontrollably. When this happens, the cancer cells can break through the surface of the ovary. It can then spread to other parts of the body.

ovaries. Glands where female reproductive cells are formed and where hormones are produced. The ovaries release an egg each month that travels down the fallopian tubes toward the uterus.

ovulation. The time when an ovary releases an egg.

pangender: An adjective describing a person whose gender identity if made up of all or many gender expressions.

panromantic. Romantic attraction towards persons of every gender.

pansexual. Those who are attracted to multiple or all ("pan") types of people, no matter what their sex or gender might be.

Pap test. A procedure used to examine the cells of the cervix in order to detect abnormal, precancerous, or cancerous growths. It is also called a Pap smear.

pelvic inflammatory disease. An infection of a woman's internal reproductive system that can lead to sterility, ectopic pregnancy, and chronic pain. It is often caused by sexually transmitted infections, such as gonorrhea and chlamydia.

penis. Cylinder-shaped organ that consist of a head or glans and a shaft of soft, spongy tissue.

polyromantic. Romantic attraction toward multiple, but not all, genders.

polysexual. People who are attracted to more than one gender or sex but do not wish to identify as bisexual because the term implies that there are only two binary genders or sexes.

pregnancy. A condition in which a woman carries a developing offspring in her uterus. It begins with the implantation of the pre-embryo and progresses through the embryonic and fetal stages until birth, unless it is ended by miscarriage or abortion. It lasts about 9 months from implantation to birth.

premenstrual syndrome. Emotional and physical symptoms that appear a few days before and during menstruation, including depression, fatigue, feeling bloated, and irritability.

progesterone. A hormone produced in the ovaries of women that is important in the regulation of puberty, menstruation, and pregnancy.

prostitute. A person who is paid to perform sexual acts.

puberty. The period of time when preteens' and teenagers' bodies change and when the sex organs become capable of reproduction.

pubic hair. Coarse, curly hair that grows in the genital area.

pubic lice. Tiny insects that can be sexually transmitted. They live in pubic hair and cause intense itching in the genitals or anus.

queer. Someone who does not identify as straight and/or does not identify as cisgender; a nonbinary label that describes diverse gender identities and sexual orientations. The word *queer* can also be used as a way to reject the acronym "LGBT," which some people feel is restricting.

questioning. To be unsure or less certain of your sexual orientation or gender identity. People figure out their sexuality and gender identity at different points in their lives, and there's no wrong way to identify.

rape. To force another person to submit to sex acts; this is a crime.

romantic attraction. Describes an individual's pattern of romantic attraction based on a person's gender(s) regardless of one's sexual orientation.

romantic orientation. Describes an individual's pattern of romantic attraction based on a person's gender(s) regardless of one's sexual orientation. For individuals who experience sexual attraction, their sexual orientation and romantic orientation are often in alignment.

scabies. Tiny mites that can be sexually transmitted. They burrow under the skin, causing intense itching, usually at night, and small bumps or rashes that appear in dirty-looking, small curling lines, especially on the penis, between the fingers, on buttocks, breasts, wrists, and thighs, and around the navel.

scrotum. Soft muscle pouch containing and protecting the testicles.

self-image. The way one views their abilities, appearance, intelligence as well as who and what they are.

semen. Fluid containing sperm that is ejaculated during sexual excitement. Semen is composed of fluid from the seminal vesicles, fluid from the prostate, and sperm from the testes.

sext. Using a cell phone to send a sexy text message or image—often of oneself.

sexual attraction. Attraction that makes people desire sexual contact or show sexual interest in another person.

sexual harassment. Includes unwelcome sexual advances, requests for sexual favors, and other verbal, nonverbal, or physical conduct of a sexual or gender-based nature. Sexual violence is a form of sexual harassment and is a crime that must be reported to law enforcement.

sexual intercourse. Sexual activity between two people, especially penetration of the vagina, anus, or mouth.

sexual orientation. The term used to describe whether a person feels sexual desire for people of the opposite gender, same gender, or both genders.

sexuality. A great gift from God; " . . . a central aspect of being human throughout life encompasses sex, gender identities and roles, sexual orientation, eroticism, pleasure, intimacy, and reproduction."[10]

sexually transmitted infections. Infections that are spread primarily through person-to-person sexual contact, including vaginal, anal, and oral sex. STIs can also be spread through nonsexual means via blood or blood products such as needles, from mother to child during pregnancy and childbirth, and tissue transfer. Common symptoms of STIs include vaginal discharge, urethral discharge or burning in men, genital ulcers, and abdominal pain. There are more than thirty different sexually transmissible bacteria, viruses, and parasites. While most of these infections are treatable, there is no cure for genital herpes, genital warts, and HIV.

shame. "The intensely painful feeling or experience of believing that we are flawed and therefore unworthy of love and belonging—something we've

---

10 Education for Mission & Ministry Unit. *Sexuality: A Divine Gift* (New York: Domestic and Foreign Missionary Society, 1987), 4.

experienced, done, or failed to do makes us unworthy of connection."[11]

"the shot." Also known as *Depo-Provera* or *Depo*. A type of female birth control given into the muscle (in the arm or hip) and lasting 3 months; keeps the ovaries from releasing eggs.

sperm. Male reproductive cells manufactured by the testicles and ejaculated in the semen. These cells enter the female egg and begin the fertilization process. A **spermicide** is a chemical used to immobilize sperm.

sponge. The sponge is made of plastic foam and contains spermicide. It is soft, round, and about 2 inches in diameter. It has a nylon loop attached to the bottom for removal. It is inserted deep into the vagina before intercourse.

statutory rape. Legally, sexual contact between an adult and anyone who is below the age of consent (in the United States this can be 16, 17, or 18 years old depending on the state) whether or not the contact is voluntary.

syphilis. A sexually transmitted infection that can lead to disfigurement, neurological disorders, and death.

testicles. Two ball-like glands inside the scrotum that produce hormones, including testosterone. Each testicle also encloses several hundred small lobes, which contain the tiny, threadlike, seminiferous tubules that produce sperm. Also called "testes," the testicles are sensitive to the touch.

testicular cancer. Testicular cancer develops if abnormal cells in one or both of the testes grow uncontrollably. Early detection is very important. Treatment is very effective and there is a high cure rate. If untreated or detected late, it can spread to other parts of the body—and it may cause death.

testosterone. An androgen that is produced in the testes of men and in smaller amounts in the ovaries of women.

trans/transgender. The "T" in LGBTQ+. Some people have a gender identity that does not match up with their biological sex. For example, they were born with "female" sex organs (vulva, vagina, uterus), but they feel like a male. People in this community sometimes call themselves *transgender* or *trans*. Trans can also include people who do not identify with the strict male/female gender roles the world tells us we should fit into. Sometimes people who do not feel either male or female call themselves *genderqueer*. (*Note:* Terms like *transgendered*, *tranny*, or *he-she* are old-fashioned and hurtful.)

transition. A person's process of developing and assuming a gender expression to match their gender identity. Transition can include: coming out to one's family, friends, and/or co-workers; changing one's name and/or sex on legal documents; hormone therapy; and possibly (though not always) some form of surgery. It's best not to assume how one transitions as it is different for everyone.

transvestite. A term that has fallen out of favor and has been replaced by cross-dresser, to describe one who dresses in clothes typical of the opposite sex but does not necessarily live as that sex.

trichomoniasis. Trichomoniasis is an infection caused by a protozoan — a microscopic, one-celled animal called a trichomona. Trichomoniasis is often called "trich."

tubal sterilization. Surgical blocking of the fallopian tubes that is intended to provide permanent birth control.

urinary tract infection (UTI). A bacterial infection of the bladder (also called "cystitis"), the ureters, or the urethra.

uterus. The pear-shaped, muscular reproductive organ from which women menstruate and where normal pregnancy develops. Also called the "womb."

vagina. The stretchable passage that connects a woman's outer sex organs, the vulva, with the cervix and uterus. The vagina has three functions: to allow menstrual flow to leave the body, to allow sexual penetration to occur, and to allow a fetus to pass through during vaginal delivery.

vaginitis. Inflammation of the vulva and/or vagina, caused by a change in the balance of vaginal bacteria, which may be caused by vaginal intercourse or manual sex play, especially with a new partner.

vas deferens. A long, narrow tube that carries sperm from each epididymis to the seminal vesicles during ejaculation. The plural of *vas deferens* is *vasa deferentia*.

vasectomy. Surgical blocking of the vasa deferentia in men that is intended to provide permanent birth control.

virgin. A person who has never had sexual intercourse. This term can be applied to both males and females. The status of never having had sexual intercourse is called **virginity**.

vulva. A woman's external sex organs, including the clitoris, labia (majora and minora), opening to the vagina (*introitus*), opening to the urethra, and two Bartholin's glands.

withdrawal. Pulling the penis out of the vagina before ejaculation in order to avoid pregnancy. A reversible, behavioral method of birth control.

womb. Refers to the uterus; often found in the Bible.

yeast infection. Usually, a type of vaginitis caused by an overgrowth of the yeast, *candida albicans*. Yeast infections may also occur in the penis or scrotum. When they occur orally, they are referred to as "thrush."

WEB RESOURCES

The Center for Lesbian & Gay Studies in Religion and Ministry: Has a mission to advance the well-being of lesbian, gay, bisexual, queer, and transgender people and to transform faith communities and the wider society by taking a leading role in shaping a new public discourse on religion, gender identity, and sexuality through education, research, community building, and advocacy. http://clgs.org

The Coalition for Positive Sexuality: Offers information in English and Spanish for young people who are sexually active or considering sexual activity. http://positive.org

Common Sense Media: A trusted media education resource offers questions and answers regarding privacy and the internet. www.commonsensemedia.org/privacy-and-internet-safety

Integrity USA: An organization "proclaiming God's inclusive love in and through the Episcopal Church since 1975. www.integrityusa.org

Iwannaknow: For youth who desire to learn about sexual health to make healthy decisions. www.iwannaknow.org

Planned Parenthood: For nearly 100 years, Planned Parenthood has promoted a commonsense approach to women's health and well-being, based on respect for each individual's right to make informed, independent decisions about health, sex, and family planning. This link offers info for teens: www.plannedparenthood.org/teens.

Sex Etc: Provides peer-to-peer education and communication. http://sexetc.org/

Stop Bullying: Information, videos, lessons, and more to respond to bullying. www.stopbullying.gov

Trans Student Educational Resources: A youth-led organization dedicated to transforming the educational environment for trans and gender nonconforming students through advocacy and empowerment. www.transstudent.org

The Trevor Project: A 24-hour hotline for teens, especially those who are LGBTQ+ and might be suicidal. www.thetrevorproject.org

Printed in the USA
CPSIA information can be obtained
at www.ICGtesting.com
JSHW012014040324
58553JS00016B/481